MW00745212

101 Fun Ways to Build Self Confidence

(For Women Volume 1)

(signature) 2011

101 Fun Ways to Build Self Confidence

(For Women Volume 1)

Terran Lamp

OUR **little** BOOKS 1

All illustrations provided by Daniel Asare Jr.,
danielasarejr@yahoo.com

The publication is designed to provide accurate and authoritative information in regard to the subject matter covered. It is sold with the understanding that the Publisher is not engaged in rendering legal, medical, accounting or other professional services. If legal or medical advice or other expert assistance is required, the services of a competent professional person should be sought. This book is not intended to treat or diagnose any medical condition and does not substitute for medical treatment. For any health difficulties and for on-going care, please see your physician, psychotherapist or other licensed medical professional.

www.ourlittlebooks.com
E-mail: sales@ourlittlebooks.com
Printed in Canada.

Introduction:

101 Fun Ways to Build Self Confidence (For Women Volume 1) offers ideas on how to be confident in your everyday life. Read it before your next job interview, your first date or your final exam. Whether you are a mother, daughter, wife, sister, niece or grandmother (or you have a mother, daughter, wife, sister, niece or grandmother), confidence is the key to success and making your wildest dreams come true!

The goal of *101 Fun Ways to Build Self Confidence* is NOT to offer complex strategies, but easy ways women can practice being confident by simply trying one idea a day or even weekly. You don't have to try all the ideas at once, just pick one until you master it and then move on to another if that is your pace. Refer to the ideas often enough so, after a while, what you have tried becomes second nature and your confidence will continue to rise.

Every 10 pages you will find 2 blank pages for your Confidence Journal. Write down the ideas you've tried. How have they worked for you? What would you change? Add your own ideas about Building Self Confidence. Looking back to your own Confidence WINS is a great way to Build Self Confidence.

(MEN! We know Self Confidence is important to you too, so your 101 Ways are coming soon in Volume 2!)

Dedication:

To MY Sisters, Mother, Nieces, Grand-mothers, Girlfriends and YOU! This is for all of us who have overcome and who are still working on our own battles to be Self Confident. DON'T give in and most certainly DON'T give up! Be the Confidence Captain of your own ship. Take control of your own destiny. Building Self Confidence is an ongoing process that doesn't always come overnight, but with true love of thyself you can obtain it.

MY GIRLS:

Brenda Lamp
Winter Lamp
Jessica Lamp
Eva Lamp
Alma Mauck

101 Fun Ways!

Every day, in every way,
I'm getting better and better.

Émile Coué

1. Smile at everyone you see for an entire day! You can't help feeling happy and confident when you smile!

2. Buy something new for yourself today!

3. Get a manicure and pedicure! Pamper yourself!

4. Make sure to put on your lip gloss before you leave the house.

5. Buy a journal and make sure you write in it! Writing allows you to express your deepest feelings and relieves stress.

6. Wash your car inside and out! It will run better and you will feel better!

7. If you can. take a mid-day nap. By tuning out for a little bit you will come back more rested and confident about the second half of your day!

8. Read a new book of your choice!

9. Try a new nail polish color! GO BOLD! Your hands are noticed more than you would think.

10. Listen to a book on CD. Learn something while driving.

11. Pay off a credit card! Your confidence will soar!

12. Get a new haircut!

13. Buy your co-worker lunch.

14. Send your mother a card! She will be surprised when it shows up and you will feel good inside.

15. Try a new style for a day! Wear something you would normally never wear!

16. Make a delicious meal for your family! Ask your children what they want!

17. Be open to trying a new food! Try something from a different culture!

18. Listen to your favorite Music CD! Make it something upbeat and sing-a-long!

19. Put money into your savings account! If you don't have a savings. START ONE!

20. Wear your best fitting pair of jeans!
Feel Sexy!

21. Set goals!
     3 mos. 6 mos. 1 yr. 5 yr. 10 yr.

22. Exercise 4-5 x Week!

23. Take care of your skin! Physical appearance isn't everything but looking good (to yourself) does play an important role in your confidence.

24. Allow yourself 15 minutes of quiet time a day. Your mind will relax and you will be more energized!

25. Keep a food log for one week and practice better eating habits!

Confidence Journal

_____

_____

_____

_____

_____

_____

_____

_____

_____

_____

_____

_____

_____

Confidence Journal

_____

_____

_____

_____

_____

_____

_____

_____

_____

_____

_____

_____

Don't compromise yourself.
You are all you've got.

Janis Joplin

26. Walk fast! You will feel important!

27. Confidence shines when you have a positive attitude!

28. Create a budget! You will feel more confident about your financial future.

29. Surround yourself with people who have MORE (financially. emotionally. mentally) than you! See where you want to be! <u>Don't be jealous</u>. it's about GROWTH!

30. Start a new hobby! Take up knitting. running or art!

31. Hang around people who have confidence! It will rub off on you!

32. Travel-Even if it is just for a WEEK-END GET-A-AWAY!

33. Play games! Board games and Video games can exercise your mind and con-fident friendly competition never hurts!

34. Learn to garden! You will be one with nature and create an amazing masterpiece!

35. Carry your favorite purse: Have you ever noticed when you have your best bag you feel great?

36. Flirt! I'm serious! I didn't say marry the man! Just flirt! It makes you feel womanly and feminine!

37. Change the shade of your eye shadow. Change is good and you will feel like a new woman.

38. Paint a room in your apartment or house! Your attitude will spark and you will feel accomplished!

Success Story 1

I spent so much time in my life wishing I had long hair. Years ago when I was complaining about my hair, this co-worker of mine said to me in her very thick Asian accent, "God has given you everything you need."

Recently I recalled that conversation and decided that she was absolutely right. God has given me everything I need. My hair is enough. My hair is actually quite beautiful. Ever since then, I've been getting everything I ever wanted and stopped letting the silly thought that my hair was too short get in the way of my goals.

So whatever your *silly* thought is, let it go and remember "God has given you everything you need". Thank HIM for it and go accomplish all your goals. Enjoy your life.

Love, Charlene

39. Write affirmations. Always include I AM CONFIDENT!

40. Tell a joke! Laughter is the best way to cheer your spirits and make you feel better throughout the day!

41. Speak in Public! Nothing can make you feel more confident than knowing you have something to say!

42. Set boundaries! In relationships with men, women or friends setting boundaries allows you to maintain your values. Set standards and stay focused on what is important to you!

43. Trust your woman's intuition! You have it for a reason, use it and stop doubting yourself!

Confidence Journal

_____

_____

_____

_____

_____

_____

_____

_____

_____

_____

_____

Confidence Journal

_____

_____

_____

_____

_____

_____

_____

_____

_____

_____

_____

_____

_____

44. Attend a networking function. You learn from others. What can you offer to the group? Who knows you might have a skill someone else has been looking for!

45. Be a leader! Step out from the crowd! Your new role will make you feel empowered and self confident!

46. Resist the temptation to compare yourself to others! You are enough!

47. Look at the areas you are strong in! What are your strengths? How can they overcome your weaknesses?

48. Make a plan and stick with it! Follow through! Completion is a great form of flattery!

49. Give Back!! The more you give the more you receive!

50. Put on a suit! Maybe you already have a POWER suit!

*As long as you're going
to think anyway, think big.*

Donald Trump

51. Sing! Even if it is just in the shower. You will feel like a million bucks after belting your best tune!

52. Do something you've been afraid to do! How awesome will it be when you conquer your fear! For today...Be Unafraid.

53. Go to your place of spiritual comfort. Meditation or Prayer.

54. Drink water! Water makes you feel refreshed and it rejuvenates your body and soul.

55. Make a daily to-do list. If you don't complete it today, no worries. You have some great goals for tomorrow.

56. Clear out your cell phone voicemail. Delete old messages and return your calls. This will help clear your mind and keep you organized.

57. Clean your office. Eliminating clutter will make you feel better about your workspace and you will be more productive and confident.

58. Remind yourself of your dreams! Take some time to daydream about where you imagine yourself in 5 years!

59. Buy a new plant! For some reason we like plants! And when we talk to them we feel even better. You don't have to have a green-thumb. Get a cactus. It will still add life to your environment!

❋ ❋ ❋

60. Put on a wig or try hair extensions! You will feel like a new and different woman!

61. Plan your meals for the week! You will feel more control over your diet and more confident about your food choices.

62. Take care of your teeth! This one sounds crazy, but it works! A nice bright smile will make you feel more confident!

63. Watch your favorite movie. Not a tear-jerker, but your favorite feel good movie of all times!

64. Just for today...Live for this day only!

65. Act like you're confident! Fake it 'til you make it! You might even convince yourself!

Confidence Journal

_____

_____

_____

_____

_____

_____

_____

_____

_____

_____

_____

_____

Confidence Journal

_____

_____

_____

_____

_____

_____

_____

_____

_____

_____

_____

_____

66. Call an old friend. Talking to child-hood pals will give you renewed energy and confidence.

67. Stand up straight! Your body language says a lot about your confidence.

68. Be agreeable! You don't have to be a push-over to be in a good mood! This will be good for you and the people you come in contact with.

69. Buy a lottery ticket! JUST ONE! It's the anticipation of possibilities...that feels good!

70. Adjust to what is. Be Present.

71. SLEEP! Getting enough sleep is an important part of your happiness! You can't feel confident when you are tired!

Success Story 2

In 2009, I participated in my first triathlon. I have always been a very active person; swimming/biking/running should have been a natural next step with one problem; unless I am at the beach or attending a pool party, I HATE swimming.

So, for the next 9 weeks, I swam 2x a week at the gym. I was not very good and started to feel down about my progress. As each week passed, I was improving slowly but surely. Finally, the big day came.

The swim was open water and I was terrified. I kept telling myself, "Ursula you can do this! You are strong, confident, and ready". It was not pretty, but I made it across the lake. After that, I floated through the bike and the run.

Preparation and support from family and friends, gave me the self confidence "boost" that I needed to complete this difficult task.

Best, Ursula

72. Celebrate at least one WIN everyday!

73. See your challenges as opportunities!

74. Accept Compliments! Take them gladly, nicely and calmly! And respond with sincerity!

75. Pet an animal! If you don't have one, be nice to someone else's! Animals give us so much great energy. If you love animals you can't help but feel confident when you cuddle one!

Make up your mind to be happy. Learn to find pleasure in the simple things.

Robert Louis Stevenson

76. Think outside the box! Creativity produces Confidence!

77. Take control of your health. A healthy you is a more confident you!

78. Have an opinion. Know what you think even if you don't voice it.

79. Be prepared and stay ready. As they say...Stay Ready so you don't have to Get Ready!

80. Write a book! Even if this is a stretch goal! It's a really fun way to boost your confidence and share your story or knowledge!

81. Go on a trip! Solo! All by yourself!

82. Forgive others...This helps you move
forward.

83. Start your own group. Maybe a book
or cooking club or a walking group.

Confidence Journal

_____

_____

_____

_____

_____

_____

_____

_____

_____

_____

_____

_____

Confidence Journal

_____

_____

_____

_____

_____

_____

_____

_____

_____

_____

_____

_____

84. Be Thankful! Appreciate the things you have!

❀ ❀ ❀

85. If there is something you have always wanted to do-START TODAY!

86. Have Hope.

87. Teach someone else a new skill. This will enforce what you know and build confidence.

88. Admit your mistakes and learn from them.

89. Expect a miracle!

90. Change your thoughts and think CONFIDENCE!

91. Exercise Courage. Courage builds confidence one day at a time.

92. Test drive your favorite car! Be careful, but see what it feels like behind the wheel of your dream car!

❀ ❀ ❀

93. Embrace Change.

94. Learn a new word today or even once a week!

95. Discover your (hidden) talent!

96. Fix something! As women we feel really good when we challenge ourselves to do something mechanical and then it actually works when we are finished!

97. Learn a new language!

98. Offer service to a complete stranger!

99. Stop Self Criticism.

Do what you can, with what you have,
where you are.

Theodore Roosevelt

100. Never stop at 100 (100% that is). Keep going! And don't stop there....

101. You are CONFIDENT! Build your Self Confidence Everyday in Every Way!

Confidence Journal

_____

_____

_____

_____

_____

_____

_____

_____

_____

_____

_____

_____

_____

Confidence Journal

_____

_____

_____

_____

_____

_____

_____

_____

_____

_____

_____

_____

Nothing can bring you peace but yourself.

Ralph Waldo Emerson

Quote Authors:

Émile Coué

Émile Coué de Châtaigneraie (February 26, 1857 – July 2, 1926) was a French psychologist who worked in psychotherapy and self-improvement.

Janis Joplin

Janis Lyn Joplin (January 19, 1943 - October 4, 1970) who came to prominence during the rock and roll era of the 1960's, was the lead singer and songwriter for Big Brother and the Holding Company. *Rolling Stone* magazine considers her one of The Greatest 100 Singers of All Time.

Donald Trump

Donald John Trump (born June 14, 1946) is an American businessman. He is the Chairman and CEO of the Trump Organization and Founder of Trump Entertainment Resorts. Donald Trump is also Host and Executive Producer of his own NBC reality show, *The Apprentice*.

Robert Louis Stevenson

Robert Louis Balfour Stevenson (13 November 1850 – 3 December 1894) was a Scottish novelist well know for his books Treasure Island, Kidnapped and The Strange Case of Dr. Jekyll and Mr. Hyde.

Theodore Roosevelt

Theodore "Teddy" Roosevelt (October 27, 1858 – January 6, 1919) was the 26th President of the United States, a Leader of the Republican Party and Founder of the Progressive ("Bull Moose") Party of 1912. He was also known as a naturalist, explorer, hunter, author and soldier.

Ralph Waldo Emerson

Ralph Waldo Emerson (May 25, 1803 – April 27, 1882) was an American philosopher, lecturer, essayist, and poet.

Author Page

Terran Lamp is a bi-racial woman currently living in Los Angeles, CA. She was born with a congenital heart condition and had open heart surgery twice before the age of 7. Realizing life's moments are precious Terran has become the creator of her own destiny. She has taken her own struggles with confidence as a way to inspire others to love themselves.

Founder of (SCWI) SelfConfidenceWearIt.com, Terran started an "I Love Myself" brand including products and workshops. SCWI originated through the need for positive messaging and building self confidence among our community, particularly in young women.

In addition to SCWI, Terran founded THINK BIG; a Los Angeles based group that promotes women to **THINK BIG** with their finances, aspirations, and life goals. You can find out more information or contact Terran at www.SelfConfidence-WearIt.com and www.WeThinkBigLA.com.

Contact 1-866-621-4662 or Email SelfConfidenceWearIt@yahoo.com if your organization is interested in hosting a SCWI (Self Confidence Wear It) workshop in your area. Opportunities are also available to groups who want to learn more about the endless possibilities available when you THINK BIG!

Terran is also available for motivational speaking.